USBORNE SIMPLE READERS

THE
BIGGEST

Nicole Irving
Illustrated by John Shackell
Edited by Heather Amery

Language Consultant: Betty Root

Reading and Language Information Centre
Reading University, England

This is Tom and Sally with their dog, Wag.
They always go on adventures together.

They are going to look for some of the biggest
animals and things in the world.

2

They have such a surprise when they see a
St. Bernard dog. It is so much bigger than Wag.

St. Bernards are the biggest dogs on earth.

The biggest animals that ever lived on land were dinosaurs. They lived millions of years ago.

Tom and Sally visit a dinosaur park. They can hardly believe how big Brachiosaurus was.

Some dinosaurs were covered in bony plates or spikes. This was to protect them from attack.

Tyrannosaurus Rex attacked other dinosaurs. It was the biggest meat eater that ever lived.

Tom and Sally go to a country show to see some of the biggest fruit and vegetables ever grown.

Sally runs away when an enormous pumpkin nearly hits her.

Tom and Sally go to the airport to get on a plane. A very long bicycle stops by their taxi.

The biggest car in the world has parked nearby. It has sixteen wheels and fifty people can sit in it.

In the distance, they see the biggest plane that has ever flown. Even helicopters can go inside.

Before they get on their plane, Tom and Sally stop to look at a giant dump truck.

In Africa they find ostriches, the biggest of all birds.
They cannot fly, but they run very fast.

Ostriches lay bigger eggs than any other bird.
The eggs have very strong shells.

Bald eagles build the biggest nests. They are so big, owls often live in them as well.

The biggest flying bird is a wandering albatross. It can spend days gliding on the wind over the sea.

In Alaska, they see a Kodiak bear.

Then, in Africa, they see a family of gorillas.

African elephants are the biggest animals that live on land. Their trunks are very useful.

Tom and Sally find some giraffes. They are the tallest animals and can eat leaves from the tops of trees.

Giraffes are gentle but they can defend themselves. They can kill a lion with one kick.

Tom and Sally are hiding. They can see a huge anaconda. It is the biggest snake in the world.

It can swallow a big meal in just one mouthful.

Then, it can go without food for two weeks.

Tom and Sally find the biggest crocodiles.
They have strong jaws and are very dangerous.

The biggest lizards on earth are called Komodo
dragons. They eat wild pigs.

Tropical stick insects are the longest insects in the world. They look like sticks.

Tom and Sally find some goliath beetles in a jungle in Africa. They are the biggest insects.

The biggest frog in the world, the biggest snail and the longest millipede also live in Africa.

The biggest spiders live in South America.
They are called bird-eating spiders.

Tom and Sally go to sea and find a blue whale.
It is the biggest animal in the world.

Blue whales eat lots and lots of tiny sea animals.
Food for one day would fill four trucks.

Whales come up to the top of the water to breathe. They have a special blowhole instead of a nose.

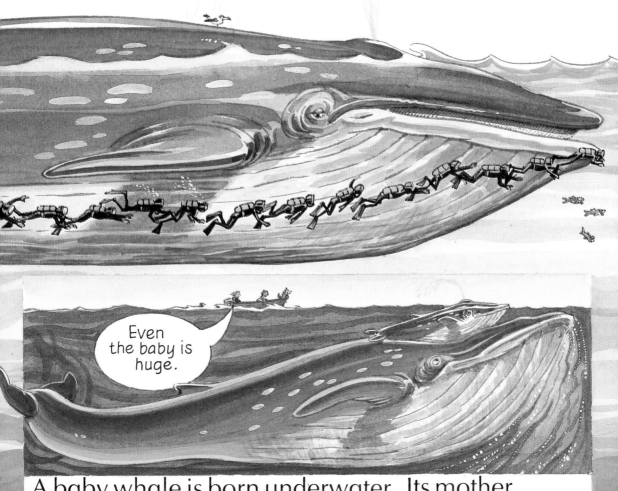

A baby whale is born underwater. Its mother quickly pushes it up so it can breathe.

Under the sea, they find a giant lobster. It is so big, its claws are as long as Sally's arms.

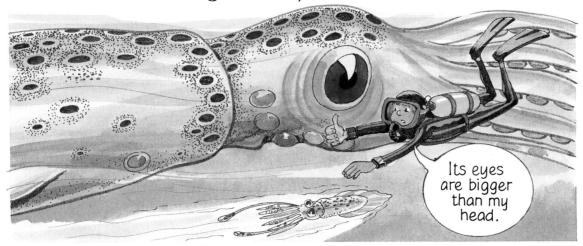

Then a giant squid swims past.
It has the biggest eyes in the world.

Tom gets a fright when he meets a giant octopus.
It has eight arms, each with hundreds of suckers.

An octopus likes eating crabs. Even crabs hiding in
between rocks are not safe from its long arms.

In the jungle, they find the biggest flower.

It smells very bad, so they run away.

Then they find the biggest water lilies in the world. They grow on the Amazon river.

Tom and Sally go to America to look for the biggest cactus and the tallest tree.

They ride into the desert to see a giant saguaro.

From a helicopter, they look at a redwood tree.

23

Tom and Sally unpack all the big shells they have brought home. Their big adventure is over.

First published in 1987. Usborne Publishing Ltd, 20 Garrick Street, London WC2E 9BJ, England. © Usborne Publishing Ltd, 1987.

American edition 1987